Roundy & Friends
Brazil

Special Edition

Andres Varela

Illustrations and Graphic Design by Carlos F. González
Co-Producer Germán Hernández
© 2019 Soccertowns® LLC

The group takes a direct flight from New York to Sao Paulo, the flying time is about 10 hours. In Sao Paulo, they take a connection flight to Salvador.

Brazil is the largest country in South America. It's located Southeast of the United States, below the Equator. Brazil has a population of 210 Million People and most of them are crazy about soccer. The country has produced some of the best soccer players in the world.

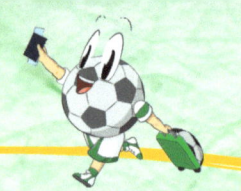

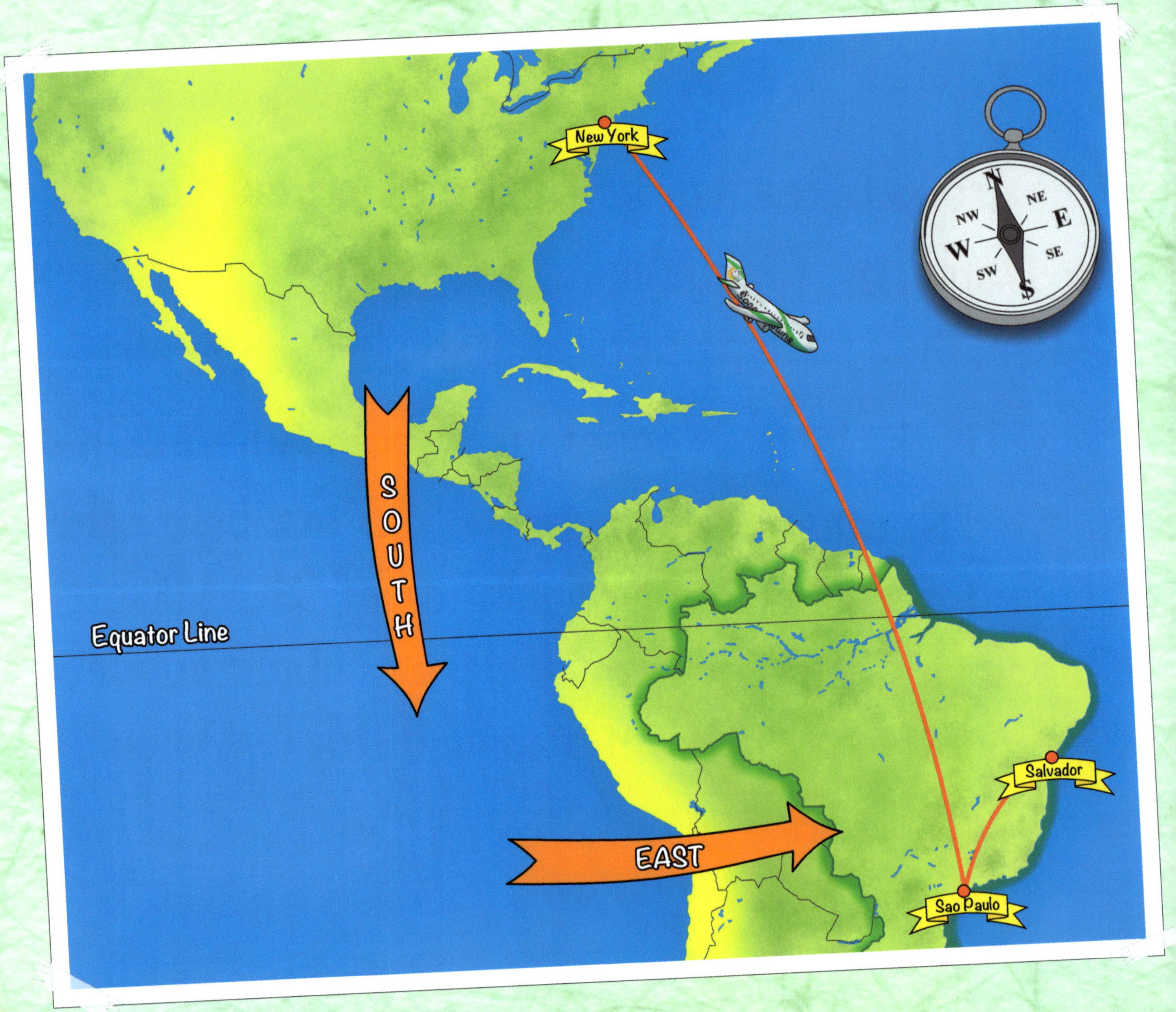
New York
N
NE
E
SE
S
SW
W
NW
SOUTH
Equator Line
Salvador
EAST
Sao Paulo

Teo explains to them the route they will take.

They plan to visit 5 cities where a championship is being held so they will be able to watch a few games and see some of the greatest soccer on the planet.

In Salvador, the team was driven by a Brazilian driver, who, luckily spoke English, in addition to his native Portuguese, which is the language spoken in Brazil.

Salvador has a population of 3.9 Million people in the metropolitan area. The city is located on the Atlantic Ocean.

The average temperature in Salvador all year long is 77 degrees Fahrenheit or 22 degrees Celsius. "Perfect time for a swim!" scream Ben and Gabe.

Beach soccer is a type of soccer commonly played in Brazil since the 1950's.

It's fast and each goal is scored on average every 3 or 4 minutes.

As they played, they could see Barra Lighthouse, one of the most iconic locations in the city. Lighthouses have been used for hundreds of years to guide boats coming toward shore from the ocean.

Fonte Nova Arena

Colombia **VS** Argentina

Belo Horizonte has a population of 2.5 Million people. It's the first planned modern city in Brazil

Founding the city in 1897

1970's

Now

After some fun in Salvador, the team travels Southwest to the next Brazillian city Belo Horizonte.

Raimundo Sampaio Stadium

Argentina VS Paraguay

Mineirão Stadium

There are 2 professional stadiums in the city.

Belo Horizonte

LAKE PAMPULHA

The team visits Serra do-Rola Moca State Park. Whee! said Roundy as he and others played in the waterfalls.

After a fun time in Belo Horizonte and swimming in the river waterfalls, they head to Rio de Janeiro.

Rio de Janeiro

Rio de Janeiro is the second largest city in the country.

The city is very famous for its beautiful beaches and landscapes.

Rio de Janeiro

The team stared in awe at the Christ the Redeemer statue, one of the most famous landmarks in South America. "This makes me feel small," said Roundy, staring up at the 124 ft. statue. After visiting the statue, they enjoyed a ride on the Sugarloaf Cable Car. They finished up the night by watching the Copacabana Fireworks.

Christ the redeemer

Sugarloaf Cable Car

Copacabana Fireworks

Nilton Santos Stadium

Chile VS Uruguay

Rio de Janeiro

Maracana Stadium

The next day they visited Rio de Janeiro's stadium and saw Chile play Uruguay at Maracana Stadium.

After the game the team saw some Capoeira artists.

Capoeira is of Afro-Brazilian origin and combines agile dance moves with unarmed combat techniques.

Capoeira in Portuguese literally means "chicken coop". Roundy was very impressed and he asked them to teach him some moves.

They head West to Sao Paulo.

Sao Paulo 100 years ago

The city has grown considerably in the last 100 years.

Sao Paulo Now

Monument to the Bandeiras

Sao Paulo is the largest city in Brazil with a population of over 12.1 Million people. It is also the largest Portuguese speaking city in the world.

The team travelled through the Octávio Frias de Oliveira Bridge. "This is beautiful," said Emma.

Octávio Frias de Oliveira Bridge

Brazilian Rodizio Steakhouses or Churrasco are common in Brazil. Different types of meat are cooked in rotating sticks and served to customers in waves.

Roundy ate 14 pieces of meat because it kept coming and coming! "I can't believe your appetite," said Teo!

Arena Corinthians

Peru VS Brazil

Brazil VS Bolivia

Morumbi Stadium

After having a great time in Brazil's largest city, the team drives Southwest to their final Brazilian city, Porto Alegre.

Porto Alegre's name could be translated as "Happy Port" in English. The city's population is just under 1.5 Million people.

Porto Alegre is located right next to the Guaiba River, which looks like a giant lake.

They take a nice walk along the water in Farroupilha Park.

Farroupilha Park

They finished their tour watching the match between Uruguay and Japan at the Arena Do Gremio.

The team covered 3,422 kilometers or 2,126 Miles on this trip. They learned many things by visiting the largest country in South America and the largest Portuguese speaking country in the world. They now know how crazy the Brazilian people are about soccer, they tasted some of the best steaks they've ever had, and they played soccer on some of the most beautiful beaches in the world. Brazil has been so much fun... See you in our next Adventure!

www.ingramcontent.com/pod-product-compliance
Lightning Source LLC
Chambersburg PA
CBHW041502220426
43661CB00016B/1230